James Weldon Johnson

GOD'S TROMBONES

James Weldon Johnson (1871–1938) was a novelist, poet, lawyer, editor, and ethnomusicologist, and the coauthor (with his brother, J. Rosamond Johnson) of the hymn "Lift Every Voice and Sing," which is widely known in the United States as the Black national anthem. Born in Jacksonville, Florida, Johnson was educated at Atlanta University and Columbia University and was the first Black lawyer admitted to the Florida Bar. He was also a songwriter in New York, the American consul in Venezuela and Nicaragua, the executive secretary of the NAACP, and a professor of creative literature at Fisk University. Johnson's books include the influential novel *The Autobiography of an Ex-Colored Man*; an autobiography, *Along This Way*; and the poetry collection *God's Trombones*.

GOD'S TROMBONES

Seven Negro Sermons in Verse

James Weldon Johnson

Illustrations by Aaron Douglas
Lettering by C. B. Falls
Introduction by Gregory Pardlo

VINTAGE CLASSICS
VINTAGE BOOKS
A DIVISION OF PENGUIN RANDOM HOUSE LLC
NEW YORK

FIRST VINTAGE CLASSICS EDITION 2023

Introduction copyright © 2023 by Gregory Pardlo

The Library of Congress has cataloged the Viking Press
   edition as follows:
Names: Johnson, James Weldon, 1871–1938.
Title: God's trombones : seven Negro sermons in verse /
   by James Weldon Johnson ; drawings by Aaron Douglas ;
   lettering by C. B. Falls.
Description: First edition. | New York : The Viking press, 1927.
Identifiers: LCCN 27012269
Subjects: LCSH: African Americans—Poetry.
Classification: LCC PS3519.O2625 G6 1927
LC record available at https://lccn.loc.gov/27012269

Vintage Classics Trade Paperback ISBN: 978-0-593-46881-4
eBook ISBN: 978-0-593-46882-1

Book design by Nicholas Alguire

vintagebooks.com

Printed in the United States of America
10 9 8 7 6 5 4 3 2 1

To Arthur B. Spingarn

CONTENTS

INTRODUCTION TO THE
VINTAGE CLASSICS EDITION (2023)

O black slave singers, gone, forgot, unfamed,
You—you alone, of all the long, long line
Of those who've sung untaught, unknown, unnamed,
Have stretched out upward, seeking the divine.
"O Black and Unknown Bards" (1922)

Ethical questions are likely to haunt any poet today who uses a mask to represent a culture. By *mask*, I mean a voice that, in the pretense of the poem, belongs to someone or something other than the poet. The mask itself is not the problem. Persona poetry is an entire genre founded on masking. However, when a poem implies its mask captures characteristics that are typical of a broad demographic, that poem is almost certainly going to be read as insensitive. Or worse. A hundred years ago, many believed that, no matter how arbitrarily they may have been categorized (or by whom), groups of people *did* share essential characteristics that could be more or less accurately depicted. The more popular the depiction, the more accurate it was perceived to be. Bias hardened into truth. If you were, like James Weldon Johnson, a poet who belonged to a community that was routinely summed up with negative stereotypes, you might, like him, choose to fight fire with fire, and create positive types to counter the negative ones. The literary ethics of today would not apply.

Readers today will have to make complex adjustments to account for the historical differences and the social logic that shaped Johnson's journey in writing *God's Trombones*. When we have made such adjustments, that is, after traveling through what scholar Michelle Wright calls "epiphenomenal time," which is a kind of historical thick description that puts meat on the bones of simple timelines, we can understand the work in more than an academic sense. The point isn't to empathize with Johnson nor to turn the work into a mere history lesson. As with any prayer, however beautifully it may ring in the ear, a poem's beauty intensifies the more we can appreciate the spiritual strivings on which it is cast.

Johnson's journey in writing these poems was not necessarily arduous, but it was protracted. By his account, nearly ten years before the book's publication in 1927, he began "nursing in [his] mind" the germ of what would become this, his second book of poems, *God's Trombones*. What could account for such a long incubation period? We can safely rule out writer's block, which Johnson was not one to suffer. He described his first book, *The Autobiography of an Ex-Colored Man*, a novel widely acknowledged to be a foundational text in the Black American literary canon, as having developed rapidly in his mind, "at times, outrunning [his] speed in getting it down." Johnson says he told himself that he didn't have time to write the sermons for *God's Trombones*, that he was too busy, but even he seems to have recognized that he was using an easy excuse to cover up a more complex one. Time, or the lack of it, was rarely an obstacle for this writer who was not easily distracted. Take, for example, the title poem of his first poetry collection, "Fifty Years." An opus of forty-one quatrains in its initial draft, Johnson wrote the poem to commemorate the semicentennial of the Emancipation Proclamation. Over the course of six weeks, he composed it in the small hours of the morning in a building that barracked rowdy Marines as well as the office where he worked his day job as US consul in Nicaragua. After the poem appeared on the front page of *The New York Times*, its editors intimated that "Fifty Years" was all but a work of genius.

He was prolific in many fields and withstood pressures of all sorts. The more pronounced bullet points on Johnson's wide-ranging resumé include lawyer, school administrator, musician, poet, and essayist. In form and content, each of his books sets out to map what would be, for him, novel and unique terrain. He was not risk-averse. He thrived outside of his comfort zone. He believed in the power of reason to lead him to the truth whether that truth favored his interests or not. With unflagging energy, he used his art to address conundrums of race and its attendant brutality. Yet, writing *God's Trombones* seems to have been uniquely challenging for him. Composing poems as sermons in the composite voice of a fictional and anonymous "old-time Negro preacher" very possibly carried Johnson to the limits of his imagination. Once he fixed on the figure of the old-time preacher, he had to compose the sermons while finding ways to invest them with real emotion, a task made all the more difficult, I'm sure, by Johnson's avowed atheism.

Deceptively simple in its message and import, *God's Trombones* is uncomplicated only in the scale of its ambition. Johnson was writing at a time when the "souls of Black folks" (to borrow a phrase from Johnson's contemporary and sometimes rival W. E. B. Du Bois) were very much at stake. Arbiters of public thought, from colonial theologians (the earliest apologists for slavery) to those later mystics of vaudeville and then, Hollywood, secured their profits and authority by stoking bigotry and racial anxiety with depictions of monstrous, imbecilic, lazy, deceitful, and, above all, justifiably downtrodden people of African descent. By the twentieth century, fighting back against this centuries-long smear campaign had become an all-hands-on-deck operation for many Black artists, writers, and intellectuals.

Johnson was committed to demonstrating the merits of Black cultural expression as well as distinguishing his own work within a cultural landscape dense with competing agendas and motives. Where Langston Hughes had turned to the blues for homegrown material in his 1926 debut poetry collection *The Weary Blues*, Johnson looked to the Black church. He subscribed to no religion, but he acknowledged its value in helping people make peace with suffering and the mysteries of life. More importantly, Johnson recognized that religion played an outsize role in the lives of Black Americans. Josef Sorrett, in his book *Spirit in the Dark: A Religious History of Racial Aesthetics*, describes Johnson's mix of literary and ecclesiastic sensibilities as a "celebratory ambivalence." That is, he revered the culture of the Black church with a kind of disinterested interest, the objective eye of an artist. Influenced by other poets, by politics, and by his belief in the soft power of art to effect material change in the lives of Black people, Johnson began working out how he might "take the primitive stuff of the old-time Negro sermon and, through art-governed expression, make it into poetry." He was on a tour of the Midwest when he encountered the preacher who would finally galvanize the project.

As the leaders of Allied nations descended on Versailles to certify the world safe for democracy, terror reigned across the United States. The public torture and execution of men, women, and children, a form of racialized terror employed to maintain the social order, had become a grim feature of American life. By 1919, the National Association for the Advancement of Colored People (NAACP) recorded at least 3,224 verifiable lynchings in the US. Deepening racial animosity and the proliferation of segregation laws effectively denied Blacks access to the levers of government. Lobbying congress directly for anything but symbolic denunciations of lynching proved futile. The nascent NAACP adopted an alternative strategy of dispatching representatives across the country in a noble but ultimately failed campaign to agitate for federal protections. Johnson, the secretary of the NAACP at the time, was assigned to tour the Midwestern United States. The tour found him speaking most often at Black churches whose congregations naturally assumed him to be a man of the cloth. Because he had previously served as US consul to Venezuela and Nicaragua, small-town newspapers heralding the prestigious visitor, as well as any locals who had the honor of introducing Johnson to audiences along the tour, often referred to him as "ex-minister to Venezuela and Nicaragua." As he explained, many people took *minister* to be synonymous with *preacher*. At one engagement, he was nearly prevented from speaking when he corrected the misunderstanding. Johnson had to reassure the church elder that elements of his presentation indeed had a "spiritual bearing" worthy of God's house.

Because its congregants' daily lives lacked the most fundamental civil protections, the Black church was more than a spiritual oasis. In addition to being a house of worship, it traditionally served as a kind of town hall. It safeguarded the well-being of its members in very tangible ways. In Johnson's posthumously published *Negro Americans, What Now?*, he describes the Black church as a "tremendous social force," and in terms he had similarly used to describe the old-time preacher: "When there was no other agency to do it, the church brought about cohesion and stabilization in a bewildered and leaderless mass." With its congregants prevented from voting and denied access to municipal services and public resources, the church, Black America's bedrock institution, became the site of civic planning and administration. Du Bois, a founding member of the NAACP, describes the Black church as "the central clubhouse of a community." Du Bois writes:

"Various organizations meet here,—the church proper, the Sunday-school, two or three insurance societies, women's societies, secret societies, and mass meetings of various kinds. Entertainments, suppers, and lectures are held beside the five or six regular weekly religious services. Considerable sums of money are collected and expended here, employment is found for the idle, strangers are introduced, news is disseminated and charity distributed." (*The Souls of Black Folk*)

For much of the twentieth century, it was unusual for anyone in a Black community not to be a member of a church. Indeed, as Du Bois says, the Black church "antedates the Negro home." In keeping with the patriarchal structure of the home, civic leaders, men like Johnson, typically *were* members of the clergy.

One of the few paths to leadership in Black communities ran through the church. Du Bois suggests that the leaders of Black churches were some of the most powerful Black people in the world. As he writes in his essay, "Of the Faith of the Fathers," from *The Souls of Black Folk*, "The Preacher is the most unique personality developed by the Negro on American soil." On this score, Johnson agrees, granting that the old-time preacher was often "a man of positive genius." Johnson's father, a respected figure in his hometown of Jacksonville, Florida, was a preacher. Had it not been for his parents' liberality, Johnson may have become a preacher, too, as it was his maternal grandmother's "burning ambition" for him to enter the clergy. No matter how awkward Johnson may have felt in that moment as he approached the pulpit after having been mistaken for a preacher, he understood the performance expected of him.

He knew the rhythm, the rhetoric, and the style. He knew, as we still know today, the patterns of call and response. He knew the stomp and the hand clap, and the way the human voice can be made to evoke entire spectrums of sound in the compass of a single note. Johnson also knew how, with limited alternatives, generations of Black Americans built upon the oral traditions that kidnapped Africans had carried with them through the Middle Passage. Early Black preachers had been expert in translating the world of the Good Book to people for whom books were often foreign, if not illicit, objects. For them, the less a sermon appealed to the logic of the page, and the more it appealed to the experience of the body, the more effective it became.

Only a generation before Johnson, Walt Whitman mined the oratory style of itinerant preachers to sing the body electric. First published in 1855, by the time it reached Johnson, *Leaves of Grass* was revered and reviled, and had made its indelible mark on the American canon. In his autobiography, *Along this Way*, Johnson describes his first encounter, around the turn of the century, with Whitman. He was writing poems in Negro dialect while keeping a lookout for alternatives to the form he would grow to detest. He writes:

"I was engulfed and submerged by [*Leaves of Grass*], and set floundering again. I felt that nothing I had written, with exception of the hymn for the Lincoln celebration, rose above puerility. I got a sudden realization of the artificiality of conventionalized Negro dialect poetry; of its exaggerated geniality, childish optimism, forced comicality, and mawkish sentiment; of its limitation as an instrument of expression to but two emotions, pathos and humor, thereby making every poem either only sad or only funny."

This encounter with Whitman strengthened Johnson's resolve to lose the racist clamp on the American tongue, and he began to see more clearly the old-time preacher as the figure through whom "the people of diverse languages and customs who were brought here from diverse parts of Africa and thrown into slavery were given their first sense of unity and solidarity." Whereas Whitman embellished his secular wisdom with the cadences of Revivalist preachers, Johnson adapted his metaphysics from the Black church. For Johnson, the preacher was an instrument of discovery and release.

There is a bit of false humility in his claim that he was merely serving as a sort of amanuensis to the figure idealized in these "seven Negro sermons in verse." Johnson had to do a good deal more than jot down a few notes—even if that is how the collection got started—while listening to a gifted preacher. There are recognizable conventions that give shape and consistency to the sermonic tradition in the Black church, but there are, as is the case in any genre of performance, as many styles as there are practitioners. Johnson's project was therefore much less clerical (pun intended) and far more creative than he allowed. The anti-urban sentiment we encounter, for example, in "The Prodigal Son," could belong to Johnson, the Victorian-era conservative, as easily as to his fictional preacher. "Babylon" lures the prodigal son away from his father's house and toward perdition. Johnson depicts the city like certain parts of newly electrified Harlem, "bright in the night-time like day, / The streets all crowded with people / . . . singing and laughing and dancing." Here, the "young man" buys a new suit and squanders his days and nights drinking, gambling, and cavorting with "the women of Babylon." The voice we encounter on the page is as much Johnson's as it is a composite of preachers Johnson studied, which is to say, it is a product of the poet's fertile imagination.

In his 1973 *Black Poets of the United States*, French scholar Jean Wagner notes that Johnson had intended to include a fictional character portrait as one of the poems comprising *God's Trombones*. Sadly, "The Reverend Jasper Jones" was not a good enough poem to warrant inclusion. If it had been included, it would have impressed upon readers that all of the sermons collected here are ultimately persona poems, and it would have given the collection a more defined speaker—the fictional Reverend Jones—to deliver the sermons. Meanwhile, the real preacher that inspired Johnson's ideal one "strode the pulpit up and down . . . and he brought into play the full gamut of his wonderful voice. . . . He intoned, he moaned, he pleaded—he blared, he crashed, he thundered." Johnson also notes the preacher's tempos, which he tried to "indicate by the line arrangement of the poems, and a certain sort of pause that is marked by a quick intaking and an audible expulsion of the breath . . . indicated by dashes." Even today, we recognize that gasp as a staple flourish of Black oratory in America. Zora Neale Hurston records it as a punctuating "ha!" at the ends of lines in a sermon included in her posthumous essay collection, *The Sanctified Church*. The gasp is a sibling to the chain gang's grunt, "hunh," in Sterling Brown's 1932 poem, "Southern Road." Johnson praises the "decided syncopation of speech . . . The rhythmical stress of this syncopation . . . obtained by a marked silent fraction of a beat . . . frequently filled in by a hand clap." This was the preacher, and the culture the preacher anchored, that Johnson sought to memorialize.

Johnson's claim that "The old-time Negro preacher is rapidly passing" is questionable. The Great Migration had inspired fears that the old folkways would be lost to urban attitudes as Black folks abandoned rural life in pursuit of opportunities in the various "Babylons" of America. As Black folks left the fields and plantations of the American South, however, their clergy and its unique style of preaching moved with them. The "old-time Negro preacher" turns up everywhere in Black cultural expression, particularly in our literature, because the spiritual aesthetic of the church has permeated all aspects of our cultural lives. Sorrett explains, "[T]he very organizing logics, aesthetic practices, and political aspirations of the African American literary tradition have been decidedly religious." He adds pointedly, "[B]lack literature is religious."

The prognosis that the old-time preacher was a dying breed of public intellectual may have contained a bit of wishful thinking. In a gesture that seemingly thanks the old-time preacher for his service while hinting that his service will no longer be required, Johnson advocates a kind of gentrification of the church by "well-educated and progressive youth" (*Negro Americans, What Now?*). "The day of the ignorant preacher," Johnson writes more decisively, "is gone." Hastening toward the dawn of a new Black church, Johnson imagines a pulpit staffed with college-educated youth committed to the institution and adept at ministering to the community's needs, secular and divine. Ultimately, the old-time Negro preacher Johnson fits on the page is a kind of transitionary figure best understood as a counterpart to Alaine Locke's New Negro. Seemingly, the former faces the past while the latter faces the future. But they are both future-oriented. That Johnson reaches back in time to find his exemplar tells us something of his priorities in advancing the agenda for civil rights. Johnson is not willing to risk Black Americans' stake in the soul of the nation—its wealth, culture, ethos, and identity—by starting afresh. The old-time preacher maintains a quality of seniority and equity in America that the figure of the New Negro lacks.

Locke, among others, conjured this protean figure associated with the Harlem Renaissance in response to demeaning stereotypes of Black people. The New Negro was educated and self-determining. The New Negro was an archetype many hoped would triumphantly eclipse the Old Negro. The drawback to simply eclipsing the Old Negro, however, was that, as a strategy, it left that demeaning stereotype in place to haunt, in ghostly relief, its more salutary successors. In other words, racist nostalgists could still resurrect the Old Negro as a comforting fantasy to evoke a happier, "great" American past. Johnson's archetype of the old-time preacher, on the other hand, served to rewrite past depictions by demonstrating more "accuracy," and thus, in the thinking of the time, made a bid for greater authenticity, that contested imaginary element upon which American social logics are founded.

Johnson's mission to elevate Black culture included a crusade against so-called Negro dialect. He praised Paul Laurence Dunbar's dialect poems, but recognized the ways that dialect reduced Black subjectivity to uniform and uncomplicated expressions, which only affirmed for anyone inclined to believe in Black inferiority that Black people were not capable of deeper, more complex feelings. For Johnson, the "instrument" of Negro dialect can only evoke either "a happy-go-lucky or a forlorn" character. "The Negro poet in the United States," Johnson states, "needs now an instrument of greater range than dialect."

The metaphor of instrumentation is central to this lifelong musician's aesthetic vision. To unpack the title of this collection is to consider those human wind instruments, the old-time Negro preachers through whom both God's breath and the poet's inspiration are transformed into proverbial music to our ears. Thus, we have to read the title as a double metaphor. The trombone represents the old-time preacher, while the preacher stands for the Black imagination. Johnson initially considered using the trumpet as the collection's central metaphor but rejected it as cliché. The trombone, as he footnotes in his introduction, is "the only wind instrument possessing a complete chromatic scale [that is] enharmonically true."

It is the trombone that possesses "the power to express the wide and varied range of emotions encompassed by the human voice." The title of this collection creates an architecture of thought that allows the old-time preacher, and by extension Black people, the widest possible range of expression.

"To place in the mouths of the talented old-time Negro preachers a language that is a literary imitation of Mississippi cotton-field dialect is sheer burlesque," Johnson writes. His aversion grew out of his distaste for white performers in blackface who lampooned Black people for the vaudeville stage, where they originated the form that had come to be known as Negro dialect. But Johnson is also responding to some of his contemporaries, Black poets who were not above placing "cotton-field dialect" in the mouths of their fictional preachers. Poets, for example, like Daniel Webster Davis, two of whose poems Johnson had included in the landmark anthology he edited, *The Book of American Negro Poetry*.

Both a poet and a preacher, Davis was a racial accommodationist who—wisely, we should note—was afraid that "flaunting the scare-crow of Negro domination" would offend his white readers. By this he meant that white readers would interpret depictions of competent, self-determining Blacks as signs that, given the chance, Black people would, in an act of retaliation, replace, if not eradicate, whites as the dominant race. Davis's poems hew strictly to the formula of comedy and pathos that Johnson so abhorred. When Davis gives his poems titles like "Is Dar Wadermilluns on High?" and "Skeetin' on de Ice" (in which the preacher speculates that the Israelites fleeing Egypt were able to cross the Red Sea because it was frozen), it's not to faithfully portray Black Americans. It is to assuage what he believed were his white readers' racial anxieties, through the use of racially demeaning stereotypes.

It is odd that Johnson should have to struggle at all against a reductive and homogenizing Negro dialect when what often gives Black cultural expression its richness is its ability to convey multiple meanings at once. Robert T. Kerlin's 1923 study, *Negro Poets and Their Poems*, explains that in the spirituals, "not a word . . . had but two meanings for the slave, a worldly one and spiritual one, and only one meaning, the spiritual one, for the master—who gladly saw this religious frenzy as an emotional safety-valve." And according to Amiri Baraka in *Blues People*, "Black cultural expression aims at circumlocution rather than at exact definition. The direct statement is considered crude and unimaginative; the veiling of all contents in ever-changing paraphrases is considered the criterion of intelligence and personality." Poems in the Black American tradition often follow these strategies of what today we might call, following Henry Louis Gates, Jr., *signifying*. As a rhetorical and poetic device, signifying is more dynamic than allusion but less systematic than allegory. Contrast Davis's preacher, for example, with the preacher in Dunbar's "An Ante-Bellum Sermon," another poem on the theme of Moses telling Pharaoh to "let my people go." Unlike Davis, Dunbar inhabits his character, which means we encounter the preacher unmediated, without the distancing effects of quotation marks. Dunbar's preacher is still a bit comical, but he's savvy, and we get a feel for the ironic tension between the poet and his mask. This *dramatic irony* is a hallmark of persona poetry. Like an inside joke, that is, like signifying, dramatic irony can throw readers off because it relies on subtext, innuendo, and shared cultural knowledge. Dramatic irony is most difficult to discern when the poet gives voice to an unidentifiable and/or hypothetical speaker, a "type."

Reading Dunbar's sermon, one might mistake the preacher's signifying disclaimer, "Now don't run an' tell yo' mastahs / Dat I's preachin' discontent. // 'Cause I isn't," as deference to prevailing social norms. It isn't. In fact, the disclaimer is a signal that we should take the preacher's meaning as an assertion of his very opposite intent to highlight the irreconcilable opposition between slavery and Christianity, and the slaveholders' hypocrisy in pretending otherwise. But Dunbar doesn't stop there. While he, like Johnson, harkens back to an old-time antebellum preacher, Dunbar signifies on a topical concern by having that preacher predict that the enslaved will one day be recognized as full citizens.

Similarly, Johnson signifies in *God's Trombones*, albeit with less bite. He employs this device with restraint in his treatment of the same theme, "Let My People Go." Here, Johnson's preacher imagines the dialogue between God and Moses. "And God said to Moses: / I've seen the awful suffering / Of my people down in Egypt / I've watched their hard oppressors, / *Their overseers and drivers*" (emphasis added). If we were unaware of how the story of Moses leading the Israelites to freedom is traditionally coded in the Black church, Johnson reveals this subtext by placing two of the most fearsome and despised figures on a slave plantation under Pharaoh's command. That Johnson signifies on an association that would have been considered a given in the Black community suggests Johnson wants white readers to register the point as well.

Furthermore, when God in Johnson's poem tells Moses to "go down, / Go down yonder into Egypt land" where "Old Pharoah" is holding God's people in bondage, the preposition is ironically multidimensional. "Down" situates us vertically as God is presumably up in heaven. "Down" in Black vernacular can also point in any cardinal direction within a local radius. But "down" in a geographic sense signifies movement south from the Mason–Dixon line, figuratively situating Pharaoh deep within slaveholding territory. Johnson's "Let My People Go" has a message for its time. Johnson is not concerned with protecting some of his readers' feelings. On the contrary, he addresses those who have inherited the wealth derived from slave labor in America as "All you sons of Pharaoh," and asks how long they think they can hold God's people—Black people by implication—down when "God himself has said, / Let my people go?"

My references to Johnson's archetypal preacher have used a masculine pronoun exclusively. This is not to reinforce a masculine norm nor is it in surrender to the conventions of Johnson's era. Rather, I hope the exclusion will highlight the extent to which women were erased from the collective imagination by some of our most influential poets and writers. Leaving it to Johnson, we might think women were relegated to minor, marginal roles within the Black church. This couldn't be further from the truth.

Thought of as an exclusively female space, the famed "amen corner," as it is popularly called, is the set of pews where women of the congregation sit, stand, shout, stomp, dance, and catch the spirit. When the preacher asks for an "amen," the amen corner obliges. It is also the case that "the prayer leader" in the Black church "was sometimes a woman." As Johnson acknowledges, "It was the prayer leader who directly prepared the way for the sermon." True, women were less likely to have been given direct access to the pulpit, but women gave the pulpit its prominence and sway. While history records the names of distinguished Black clergymen like Bishop Daniel Payne, James W. C. Pennington, Samuel R. Ward, Henry Highland Garnet, US Senator Hiram R. Revels, and many many others, we are left to imagine the lives of women who claimed recognition as preachers.

Think of Sojourner Truth and the lesser-known Nannie Burroughs, women whose faith and leadership suited them for the pulpit, but whose indomitable spirit had to find its outlet in political activism. Thanks to Lydia Maria Child, the famed editor of Harriet Jacob's *Incidents in the Life of a Slave Girl*, we do have a glimpse of an old-time Black woman preacher. The daughter of a man who had escaped slavery, Julia Pell was the kind of illiterate theologian that Davis would have found troubling. In a letter dated December 9, 1841, Child describes Pell, whom she encountered in Philadelphia. Having attended Pell's sermon one Sunday, Child writes:

"Such an odd jumbling together of all sorts of things in Scripture, such wild fancies, beautiful, sublime, or grotesque, such vehemence of gesture, such dramatic attitudes, I never before heard and witnessed. I verily thought [Pell] would have leaped over the pulpit; and if she had, I was almost prepared to have seen her poise herself on unseen wings, above the wondering congregation" (*Letters from New York*).

Child further described Pell's "wild fancies" as "purely her own idea." Another way of putting it, Pell's sermon was the product of a poetic imagination that, had they witnessed it together, Davis and Johnson may equally have found it indecorous. Child not only recognized Pell's sermon as "beautifully poetic." She found it "not unworthy of Milton."

Accounting for biases, hyperboles, and competing claims to authenticity, we might begin to understand the historical context Johnson is responding to when he writes *God's Trombones*, but our understanding should not exempt him from criticism attuned to our own era. When we measure *God's Trombones* neither to condemn nor to vindicate it against the moral and aesthetic standards of today, we give it dimension. We extend its life and the lives imagined within it. No text is perfect, but every text reflects something of the historical moment that shaped it. In this way, we inherit the old-time preachers and poets, those known and unknown who are, like us, as flawed as the standards we use to evaluate them. We must be informed readers without surrendering to the authority of a poem or even to our interpretations of it.

Just as important as what a poem means is how we give it meaning. By sharpening these practices against the stone of time we can begin to imagine futures that we might look forward to inhabiting together.

Gregory Pardlo
October 2022

Gregory Pardlo is the author of *Digest*, winner of the 2015 Pulitzer Prize for Poetry. His other books include *Totem*, winner of the American Poetry Review/Honickman Prize, and *Air Traffic*, a memoir in essays. His honors include fellowships from the New York Public Library's Cullman Center, New York Foundation for the Arts, the National Endowment for the Arts, and the Guggenheim Foundation. He is co-director of the Institute for the Study of Global Racial Justice at Rutgers University–Camden, and currently lives with his family in the UAE where he is a visiting professor of creative writing at NYU Abu Dhabi.

REFERENCES

Baraka, Imamu Amiri. *Blues People: Negro Music in White America.* New York: Perennial, 1999.

Blount, Marcellus. "The Preacherly Text: African American Poetry and Vernacular Performance." *PMLA* 107, no. 3 (1992): 582–93. Accessed October 9, 2022. https://doi.org/10.2307/462763.

Bowen, Barbara E. "Untroubled Voice: Call-and-Response in Cane." *Black American Literature Forum* 16, no. 1 (1982): 12–18. Accessed October 9, 2022. https://doi.org/10.2307/2904267.

Carroll, Anne E. *Word, Image, and the New Negro: Representation and Identity in the Harlem Renaissance*. Bloomington, IN: Indiana University Press, 2007.

Child, Lydia M. *Letters from New York*. New York: C. S. Francis & Company, 1846.

Davis, Daniel W. *'Weh Down Souf and Other Poems*. Cleveland, OH: Helman-Taylor Company, 1897.

Davis, Gerald L. *I Got the Word in Me and I Can Sing It, You Know: A Study of the Performed African-American Sermon*. Philadelphia: University of Pennsylvania Press, 1985.

Du Bois, W. E. B. *The Souls of Black Folk*. New York: Oxford University Press, 2008.

Hill, Melanie R. "Set Thine House in Order: Black Feminism and the Sermon as Sonic Art in *The Amen Corner*." *Religions* 10, no. 4 (2019): 271. https://doi.org/10.3390/rel10040271.

Hurston, Zora N. *The Sanctified Church*. Berkeley, CA: Marlowe & Company, 1981.

Hutchinson, George. *The Harlem Renaissance in Black and White*. Cambridge, MA: The Belknap Press of Harvard University Press, 1997.

Johnson, James W. *Negro Americans, What Now?* New York: Viking Press, 1934.

Kerlin, Robert T. *Negro Poets and Their Poems*. Washington, D.C.: Associated Publishers, 1923.

Ross, Marlon B. *Manning the Race: Reforming Black Men in the Jim Crow Era*. New York: New York University Press, 2004.

Sherman, Joan R. "Daniel Webster Davis: A Black Virginia Poet in the Age of Accommodation." *The Virginia Magazine of History and Biography* 81, no. 4 (October 1973): 457–78. Accessed August 23, 2022. http://www.jstor.org/stable/4247828.

Sorett, Josef. *Spirit in the Dark: A Religious History of Racial Aesthetics*. New York: Oxford University Press, 2019.

Wagner, Jean. *Black Poets of the United States*. Chicago: University of Illinois Press, 1973.

Woodson, Carter G. *The History of the Negro Church*. Bibliotech Press, 2020.

Hear Johnson read "The Creation": https://media.sas.upenn.edu/pennsound/authors/Johnson-JW/Johnson-James-Weldon_01_533A_The-Creation_Speech-Lab-Recordings_New-York_1935.mp3

Preface

A good deal has been written on the folk creations of the American Negro: his music, sacred and secular; his plantation tales, and his dances; but that there are folk sermons, as well, is a fact that has passed unnoticed. I remember hearing in my boyhood sermons that were current, sermons that passed with only slight modifications from preacher to preacher, and from locality to locality. Such sermons were "The Valley of Dry Bones," which was based on the vision of the prophet in the 37th chapter of Ezekiel; the "Train Sermon," in which both God and the devil were pictured as running trains, one loaded with saints, that pulled up in heaven, and the other with sinners, that dumped its load in hell; the "Heavenly March," which gave in detail the journey of the faithful from earth, on up through the pearly gates to the great white throne. Then there was a stereotyped sermon, which had no definite subject and which was quite generally preached; it began with the Creation, went on to the fall of man, rambled through the trials and tribulations of the Hebrew Children, came down to the redemption by Christ, and ended with the Judgment Day and a warning and an exhortation to sinners. This was the framework of a sermon that allowed the individual preacher the widest latitude that could be desired for all his arts and powers. There was one Negro sermon that in its day was a classic, and widely known to the public. Thousands of people, white and black, flocked to the church of John Jasper in Richmond, Virginia, to hear him preach his famous sermon proving that the earth is flat and the sun does move. John Jasper's sermon was imitated and adapted by many lesser preachers.

I heard only a few months ago in Harlem an up-to-date version of the "Train Sermon." The preacher styled himself "Son of Thunder"—a sobriquet adopted by many of the old-time preachers—and phrased his subject, "The Black Diamond Express, running between here and hell, making thirteen stops and arriving in hell ahead of time."

The old-time Negro preacher has not yet been given the niche in which he properly belongs. He has been portrayed only as a semi-comic figure. He had, it is true, his comic aspects, but on the whole he was an important figure, and at bottom a vital factor. It was through him that the people of diverse languages and customs who were brought here from diverse parts of Africa and thrown into slavery were given their first sense of unity and solidarity. He was the first shepherd of this bewildered flock. His power for good or ill was very great. It was the old-time preacher who for generations was the mainspring of hope and inspiration for the Negro in America. It was also he who instilled into the Negro the narcotic doctrine epitomized in the Spiritual "You May Have All Dis World, But Give Me Jesus." This power of the old-time preacher, somewhat lessened and changed in his successors, is still a vital force; in fact, it is still the greatest single influence among the colored people of the United States. The Negro today is, perhaps, the most priest-governed group in the country.

The history of the Negro preacher reaches back to Colonial days. Before the Revolutionary War, when slavery had not yet taken on its more grim and heartless economic aspects, there were famed black preachers who preached to both whites and blacks. George Liele was preaching to whites and blacks at Augusta, Georgia, as far back as 1773, and Andrew Bryan at Savannah a few years later.* The most famous of these earliest preachers was Black Harry, who during the Revolutionary period accompanied Bishop Asbury as a drawing card and preached from the same platform with other founders of the Methodist Church. Of him, John Lednum in his *History of the Rise of Methodism in America* says, "The truth was that Harry was a more popular speaker than Mr. Asbury or almost anyone else in his day." In the two or three decades before the Civil War Negro preachers in the North, many of them well-educated and cultured, were courageous spokesmen against slavery and all its evils.

The effect on the Negro of the establishment of separate and independent places of worship can hardly

---

* See *The History of the Negro Church,* Carter G. Woodson.

be estimated. Some idea of how far this effect reached may be gained by a comparison between the social and religious trends of the Negroes of the Old South and of the Negroes of French Louisiana and the West Indies, where they were within and directly under the Roman Catholic Church and the Church of England. The old-time preacher brought about the establishment of these independent places of worship and thereby provided the first sphere in which race leadership might develop and function. These scattered and often clandestine groups have grown into the strongest and richest organization among colored Americans. Another thought—except for these separate places of worship there never would have been any Spirituals.

The old-time preacher was generally a man far above the average in intelligence; he was, not infrequently, a man of positive genius. The earliest of these preachers must have virtually committed many parts of the Bible to memory through hearing the scriptures read or preached from in the white churches which the slaves attended. They were the first of the slaves to learn to read, and their reading was confined to the Bible, and specifically to the more dramatic passages of the Old Testament. A text served mainly as a starting point and often had no relation to the development of the sermon. Nor would the old-time preacher balk at any text within the lids of the Bible. There is the story of one who after reading a rather cryptic passage took off his spectacles, closed the Bible with a bang and by way of preface said, "Brothers and sisters, this morning—I intend to explain the unexplainable—find out the undefinable—ponder over the imponderable—and unscrew the inscrutable."

The old-time Negro preacher of parts was above all an orator, and in good measure an actor. He knew the secret of oratory, that at bottom it is a progression of rhythmic words more than it is anything else. Indeed, I have witnessed congregations moved to ecstasy by the rhythmic intoning of sheer incoherencies. He was a master of all the modes of eloquence. He often possessed a voice that was a marvelous instrument, a voice he could modulate from a sepulchral whisper to a crashing thunder clap. His discourse was generally kept at a high pitch of fervency, but occasionally he dropped into colloquialisms and, less often, into humor. He preached a personal and anthropomorphic God, a sure-enough heaven and a red-hot hell. His imagination was bold and unfettered. He had the power to sweep his hearers before him; and so himself was often swept away. At such times his language was not prose but poetry. It was from memories of such preachers there grew the idea of this book of poems.

In a general way, these poems were suggested by the rather vague memories of sermons I heard preached in my childhood; but the immediate stimulus for setting them down came quite definitely at a comparatively recent date. I was speaking on a Sunday in Kansas City, addressing meetings in various colored churches. When

I had finished my fourth talk it was after nine o'clock at night, but the committee told me there was still another meeting to address. I demurred, making the quotation about the willingness of the spirit and the weakness of the flesh, for I was dead tired. I also protested the lateness of the hour, but I was informed that for the meeting at this church we were in good time. When we reached the church an "exhorter" was just concluding a dull sermon. After his there were two other short sermons. These sermons proved to be preliminaries, mere curtain-raisers for a famed visiting preacher. At last he arose. He was a dark-brown man, handsome in his gigantic proportions. He appeared to be a bit self-conscious, perhaps impressed by the presence of the "distinguished visitor" on the platform, and started in to preach a formal sermon from a formal text. The congregation sat apathetic and dozing. He sensed that he was losing his audience and his opportunity. Suddenly he closed the Bible, stepped out from behind the pulpit and began to preach. He started intoning the old folk sermon that begins with the creation of the world and ends with Judgment Day. He was at once a changed man, free, at ease and masterful. The change in the congregation was instantaneous. An electric current ran through the crowd. It was in a moment alive and quivering; and all the while the preacher held it in the palm of his hand. He was wonderful in the way he employed his conscious and unconscious art. He strode the pulpit up and down in what was actually a very rhythmic dance, and he brought into play the full gamut of his wonderful voice, a voice—what shall I say?—not of an organ or a trumpet, but rather of a trombone,* the instrument possessing above all others the power to express the wide and varied range of emotions encompassed by the human voice—and with greater amplitude. He intoned, he moaned, he pleaded—he blared, he crashed, he thundered. I sat fascinated; and more, I was, perhaps against my will, deeply moved; the emotional effect upon me was irresistible. Before he had finished I took a slip of paper and somewhat surreptitiously jotted down some ideas for the first poem, "The Creation."

At first thought, Negro dialect would appear to be the precise medium for these old-time sermons; however, as the reader will see, the poems are not written in dialect. My reason for not using the dialect is double. First, although the dialect is the exact instrument for voicing certain traditional phases of Negro life, it is, and perhaps by that very exactness, a quite limited instrument. Indeed, it is an instrument with but two complete stops, pathos and humor. This limitation is not due to any defect of the dialect as dialect, but to the mould of convention in which Negro dialect in the United States has been set, to the fixing effects of its long association with the Negro only as a happy-go-lucky or a forlorn figure. The Aframerican poet might in time be able to break this mould of convention

---

* *Trombone:* A powerful brass instrument of the trumpet family, the only wind instrument possessing a complete chromatic scale enharmonically true, like the human voice or the violin, and hence very valuable in the orchestra. —*Standard Dictionary*

and write poetry in dialect without feeling that his first line will put the reader in a frame of mind which demands that the poem be either funny or sad, but I doubt that he will make the effort to do it; he does not consider it worth the while. In fact, practically no poetry is being written in dialect by the colored poets of today. These poets have thrown aside dialect and discarded most of the material and subject matter that went into dialect poetry. The passing of dialect as a medium for Negro poetry will be an actual loss, for in it many beautiful things can be done, and done best; however, in my opinion, *traditional* Negro dialect as a form for Aframerican poets is absolutely dead. The Negro poet in the United States, for poetry which he wishes to give a distinctively racial tone and color, needs now an instrument of greater range than dialect; that is, if he is to do more than sound the small notes of sentimentality. I said something on this point in *The Book of American Negro Poetry,* and because I cannot say it better, I quote: "What the colored poet in the United States needs to do is something like what Synge did for the Irish; he needs to find a form that will express the racial spirit by symbols from within rather than by symbols from without—such as the mere mutilation of English spelling and pronunciation. He needs a form that is freer and larger than dialect, but which will still hold the racial flavor; a form expressing the imagery, the idioms, the peculiar turns of thought and the distinctive humor and pathos, too, of the Negro, but which will also be capable of voicing the deepest and highest emotions and aspirations and allow of the widest range of subjects and the widest scope of treatment." The form of "The

Creation," the first poem of this group, was a first experiment by me in this direction.

The second part of my reason for not writing these poems in dialect is the weightier. The old-time Negro preachers, though they actually used dialect in their ordinary intercourse, stepped out from its narrow confines when they preached. They were all saturated with the sublime phraseology of the Hebrew prophets and steeped in the idioms of King James English, so when they preached and warmed to their work they spoke another language, a language far removed from traditional Negro dialect. It was really a fusion of Negro idioms with Bible English; and in this there may have been, after all, some kinship with the innate grandiloquence of their old African tongues. To place in the mouths of the talented old-time Negro preachers a language that is a literary imitation of Mississippi cotton-field dialect is sheer burlesque.

Gross exaggeration of the use of big words by these preachers, in fact by Negroes in general, has been commonly made; the laugh being at the exhibition of ignorance involved. What is the basis of this fondness for big words? Is the predilection due, as is supposed, to ignorance desiring to parade itself as knowledge? Not at all. The old-time Negro preacher loved the sonorous, mouth-filling, ear-filling phrase because it gratified a highly developed sense of sound and rhythm in himself and his hearers.

I claim no more for these poems than that I have written them after the manner of the primitive sermons. In the writing of them I have, naturally, felt the influence of the Spirituals. There is, of course, no way of re-creating the atmosphere—the fervor of the congregation, the amens and hallelujahs, the undertone of singing which was often a soft accompaniment to parts of the sermon; nor the personality of the preacher—his physical magnetism, his gestures and gesticulations, his changes of tempo, his pauses for effect, and, more than all, his tones of voice. These poems would better be intoned than read; especially does this apply to "Listen, Lord," "The Crucifixion," and "The Judgment Day." But the intoning practiced by the old-time preacher is a thing next to impossible to describe; it must be heard, and it is extremely difficult to imitate even when heard. The finest, and perhaps the only demonstration ever given to a New York public, was the intoning of the dream in Ridgely Torrence's *Rider of Dreams* by Opal Cooper of the Negro Players at the Madison Square Theatre in 1917. Those who were fortunate enough to hear him can never, I know, forget the thrill of it. This intoning is always a matter of crescendo and diminuendo in the intensity—a rising and falling between plain speaking and wild chanting. And often a startling effect is gained by breaking off suddenly at the highest point of intensity and dropping into the monotone of ordinary speech.

The tempos of the preacher I have endeavored to indicate by the line arrangement of the poems, and a certain sort of pause that is marked by a quick intaking and an audible expulsion of the breath I have indicated by dashes. There is a decided syncopation of speech—the crowding in of many syllables or the lengthening out of a few to fill one metrical foot, the sensing of which must be left to the reader's ear. The rhythmical stress of this syncopation is partly obtained by a marked silent fraction of a beat; frequently this silent fraction is filled in by a hand clap.

One factor in the creation of atmosphere I have included—the preliminary prayer. The prayer leader was sometimes a woman. It was the prayer leader who directly prepared the way for the sermon, set the scene, as it were. However, a most impressive concomitant of the prayer, the chorus of responses which gave it an antiphonal quality, I have not attempted to set down. These preliminary prayers were often products hardly less remarkable than the sermons.

The old-time Negro preacher is rapidly passing. I have here tried sincerely to fix something of him.

New York City, 1927.

Listen Lord
A Prayer

LISTEN, LORD—A PRAYER

O Lord, we come this morning
Knee-bowed and body-bent
Before thy throne of grace.
O Lord—this morning—
Bow our hearts beneath our knees,
And our knees in some lonesome valley.
We come this morning—
Like empty pitchers to a full fountain,
With no merits of our own.
O Lord—open up a window of heaven,
And lean out far over the battlements of glory,
And listen this morning.

Lord, have mercy on proud and dying sinners—
Sinners hanging over the mouth of hell,
Who seem to love their distance well.
Lord—ride by this morning—
Mount your milk-white horse,

And ride-a this morning—
And in your ride, ride by old hell,
Ride by the dingy gates of hell,
And stop poor sinners in their headlong plunge.

And now, O Lord, this man of God,
Who breaks the bread of life this morning—
Shadow him in the hollow of thy hand,
And keep him out of the gunshot of the devil.
Take him, Lord—this morning—
Wash him with hyssop inside and out,
Hang him up and drain him dry of sin.
Pin his ear to the wisdom-post,
And make his words sledge hammers of truth—
Beating on the iron heart of sin.
Lord God, this morning—
Put his eye to the telescope of eternity,
And let him look upon the paper walls of time.
Lord, turpentine his imagination,
Put perpetual motion in his arms,
Fill him full of the dynamite of thy power,
Anoint him all over with the oil of thy salvation,
And set his tongue on fire.

And now, O Lord—
When I've done drunk my last cup of sorrow—
When I've been called everything but a child of God—
When I'm done travelling up the rough side of the
    mountain—

O—Mary's Baby—
When I start down the steep and slippery steps of
   death—
When this old world begins to rock beneath my feet—
Lower me to my dusty grave in peace
To wait for that great gittin' up morning—Amen.

THE CREATION

And God stepped out on space,
And he looked around and said:
I'm lonely—
I'll make me a world.

And far as the eye of God could see
Darkness covered everything,
Blacker than a hundred midnights
Down in a cypress swamp.

Then God smiled,
And the light broke,
And the darkness rolled up on one side,
And the light stood shining on the other,
And God said: That's good!

Then God reached out and took the light in his hands,
And God rolled the light around in his hands
Until he made the sun;
And he set that sun a-blazing in the heavens.
And the light that was left from making the sun
God gathered it up in a shining ball
And flung it against the darkness,
Spangling the night with the moon and stars.
Then down between
The darkness and the light
He hurled the world;
And God said: That's good!

Then God himself stepped down—
And the sun was on his right hand,
And the moon was on his left;
The stars were clustered about his head,
And the earth was under his feet.
And God walked, and where he trod
His footsteps hollowed the valleys out
And bulged the mountains up.

Then he stopped and looked and saw
That the earth was hot and barren.
So God stepped over to the edge of the world
And he spat out the seven seas—
He batted his eyes, and the lightnings flashed—
He clapped his hands, and the thunders rolled—

And the waters above the earth came down,
The cooling waters came down.

Then the green grass sprouted,
And the little red flowers blossomed,
The pine tree pointed his finger to the sky,
And the oak spread out his arms,
The lakes cuddled down in the hollows of the ground,
And the rivers ran down to the sea;
And God smiled again,
And the rainbow appeared,
And curled itself around his shoulder.

Then God raised his arm and he waved his hand
Over the sea and over the land,
And he said: Bring forth! Bring forth!
And quicker than God could drop his hand,
Fishes and fowls
And beasts and birds
Swam the rivers and the seas,
Roamed the forests and the woods,
And split the air with their wings.
And God said: That's good!

Then God walked around,
And God looked around
On all that he had made.

He looked at his sun,
And he looked at his moon,
And he looked at his little stars;
He looked on his world
With all its living things,
And God said: I'm lonely still.

Then God sat down—
On the side of a hill where he could think;
By a deep, wide river he sat down;
With his head in his hands,
God thought and thought,
Till he thought: I'll make me a man!

Up from the bed of river
God scooped the clay;
And by the bank of the river
He kneeled him down;
And there the great God Almighty
Who lit the sun and fixed it in the sky,
Who flung the stars to the most far corner of the night,
Who rounded the earth in the middle of his hand;
This Great God,
Like a mammy bending over her baby,
Kneeled down in the dust
Toiling over a lump of clay
Till he shaped it in his own image;

Then into it he blew the breath of life,
And man became a living soul.
Amen. Amen.

The Prodigal Son

THE PRODIGAL SON

Young man—
Young man—
Your arm's too short to box with God.

But Jesus spake in a parable, and he said:
A certain man had two sons.
Jesus didn't give this man a name,
But his name is God Almighty.
And Jesus didn't call these sons by name,
But ev'ry young man,
Ev'rywhere,
Is one of these two sons.

And the younger son said to his father,
He said: Father, divide up the property,
And give me my portion now.

And the father with tears in his eyes said: Son,
Don't leave your father's house.
But the boy was stubborn in his head,
And haughty in his heart,
And he took his share of his father's goods,
And went into a far-off country.

There comes a time,
There comes a time
When ev'ry young man looks out from his father's house,
Longing for that far-off country.

And the young man journeyed on his way,
And he said to himself as he travelled along:
This sure is an easy road,
Nothing like the rough furrows behind my father's plow.

Young man—
Young man—
Smooth and easy is the road
That leads to hell and destruction.
Down grade all the way,
The further you travel, the faster you go.
No need to trudge and sweat and toil,
Just slip and slide and slip and slide
Till you bang up against hell's iron gate.

And the younger son kept travelling along,
Till at night-time he came to a city.
And the city was bright in the night-time like day,
The streets all crowded with people,
Brass bands and string bands a-playing,
And ev'rywhere the young man turned
There was singing and laughing and dancing.
And he stopped a passer-by and he said:
Tell me what city is this?
And the passer-by laughed and said: Don't you know?
This is Babylon, Babylon,
The great city of Babylon.
Come on, my friend, and go along with me.
And the young man joined the crowd.

Young man—
Young man—
You're never lonesome in Babylon.
You can always join a crowd in Babylon.
Young man—
Young man—
You can never be alone in Babylon,
Alone with your Jesus in Babylon.
You can never find a place, a lonesome place,
A lonesome place to go down on your knees,
And talk with your God, in Babylon.
You're always in a crowd in Babylon.

And the young man went with his new-found friend,
And bought himself some brand new clothes,
And he spent his days in the drinking dens,
Swallowing the fires of hell.
And he spent his nights in the gambling dens,
Throwing dice with the devil for his soul.
And he met up with the women of Babylon.
Oh, the women of Babylon!
Dressed in yellow and purple and scarlet,
Loaded with rings and earrings and bracelets,
Their lips like a honeycomb dripping with honey,
Perfumed and sweet-smelling like a jasmine flower;
And the jasmine smell of the Babylon women
Got in his nostrils and went to his head,
And he wasted his substance in riotous living,
In the evening, in the black and dark of night,
With the sweet-sinning women of Babylon.
And they stripped him of his money,
And they stripped him of his clothes,
And they left him broke and ragged
In the streets of Babylon.

Then the young man joined another crowd—
The beggars and lepers of Babylon.
And he went to feeding swine,
And he was hungrier than the hogs;
He got down on his belly in the mire and mud
And ate the husks with the hogs.
And not a hog was too low to turn up his nose
At the man in the mire of Babylon.

Then the young man came to himself—
He came to himself and said:
In my father's house are many mansions,
Ev'ry servant in his house has bread to eat,
Ev'ry servant in his house has a place to sleep;
I will arise and go to my father.
And his father saw him afar off,
And he ran up the road to meet him.
He put clean clothes upon his back,
And a golden chain around his neck,
He made a feast and killed the fatted calf,
And invited the neighbors in.

Oh-o-oh, sinner,
When you're mingling with the crowd in Babylon—
Drinking the wine of Babylon—
Running with the women of Babylon—
You forget about God, and you laugh at Death.
Today you've got the strength of a bull in your neck
And the strength of a bear in your arms,
But some o' these days, some o' these days,
You'll have a hand-to-hand struggle with bony Death,
And Death is bound to win.

Young man, come away from Babylon,
That hell-border city of Babylon.
Leave the dancing and gambling of Babylon,
The wine and whiskey of Babylon,
The hot-mouthed women of Babylon;

Fall down on your knees,
And say in your heart:
I will arise and go to my Father.

GO DOWN DEATH—
A FUNERAL SERMON

Weep not, weep not,
She is not dead;
She's resting in the bosom of Jesus.
Heart-broken husband—weep no more;
Grief-stricken son—weep no more;
Left-lonesome daughter—weep no more;
She's only just gone home.

Day before yesterday morning,
God was looking down from his great, high heaven,
Looking down on all his children,
And his eye fell on Sister Caroline,
Tossing on her bed of pain.
And God's big heart was touched with pity,
With the everlasting pity.

And God sat back on his throne,
And he commanded that tall, bright angel standing at
    his right hand:
Call me Death!
And that tall, bright angel cried in a voice
That broke like a clap of thunder:
Call Death!—Call Death!
And the echo sounded down the streets of heaven
Till it reached away back to that shadowy place,
Where Death waits with his pale, white horses.

And Death heard the summons,
And he leaped on his fastest horse,
Pale as a sheet in the moonlight.
Up the golden street Death galloped,
And the hoofs of his horse struck fire from the gold,
But they didn't make no sound.
Up Death rode to the Great White Throne,
And waited for God's command.

And God said: Go down, Death, go down,
Go down to Savannah, Georgia,
Down in Yamacraw,
And find Sister Caroline.
She's borne the burden and heat of the day,
She's labored long in my vineyard,
And she's tired—
She's weary—
Go down, Death, and bring her to me.

And Death didn't say a word,
But he loosed the reins on his pale, white horse,
And he clamped the spurs to his bloodless sides,
And out and down he rode,
Through heaven's pearly gates,
Past suns and moons and stars;
On Death rode,
And the foam from his horse was like a comet in the sky;
On Death rode,
Leaving the lightning's flash behind;
Straight on down he came.

While we were watching round her bed,
She turned her eyes and looked away,
She saw what we couldn't see;
She saw Old Death. She saw Old Death
Coming like a falling star.
But Death didn't frighten Sister Caroline;
He looked to her like a welcome friend.
And she whispered to us: I'm going home,
And she smiled and closed her eyes.

And Death took her up like a baby,
And she lay in his icy arms,
But she didn't feel no chill.
And Death began to ride again—
Up beyond the evening star,
Out beyond the morning star,
Into the glittering light of glory,

On to the Great White Throne,
And there he laid Sister Caroline
On the loving breast of Jesus.

And Jesus took his own hand and wiped away her tears,
And he smoothed the furrows from her face,
And the angels sang a little song,
And Jesus rocked her in his arms,
And kept a-saying: Take your rest,
Take your rest, take your rest.

Weep not—weep not,
She is not dead;
She's resting in the bosom of Jesus.

Noah Built the Ark

NOAH BUILT THE ARK

In the cool of the day—
God was walking—
Around in the Garden of Eden.
And except for the beasts, eating in the fields,
And except for the birds, flying through the trees,
The garden looked like it was deserted.
And God called out and said: Adam,
Adam, where art thou?
And Adam, with Eve behind his back,
Came out from where he was hiding.

And God said: Adam,
What hast thou done?
Thou hast eaten of the tree!
And Adam,
With his head hung down,
Blamed it on the woman.

For after God made the first man Adam,
He breathed a sleep upon him;
Then he took out of Adam one of his ribs,
And out of that rib made woman.
And God put the man and woman together
In the beautiful Garden of Eden,
With nothing to do the whole day long
But play all around in the garden.
And God called Adam before him,
And he said to him:
Listen now, Adam,
Of all the fruit in the garden you can eat,
Except of the tree of knowledge;
For the day thou eatest of that tree,
Thou shalt surely die.

Then pretty soon along came Satan.
Old Satan came like a snake in the grass
To try out his tricks on the woman.
I imagine I can see Old Satan now
A-sidling up to the woman.
I imagine the first word Satan said was:
Eve, you're surely good looking.
I imagine he brought her a present, too,—
And, if there was such a thing in those ancient days,
He brought her a looking-glass.

And Eve and Satan got friendly—
Then Eve got to walking on shaky ground;

Don't ever get friendly with Satan.—
And they started to talk about the garden,
And Satan said: Tell me, how do you like
The fruit on the nice, tall, blooming tree
Standing in the middle of the garden?
And Eve said:
That's the forbidden fruit,
Which if we eat we die.

And Satan laughed a devilish little laugh,
And he said to the woman: God's fooling you, Eve;
That's the sweetest fruit in the garden.
I know you can eat that forbidden fruit,
And I know that you will not die.

And Eve looked at the forbidden fruit,
And it was red and ripe and juicy.
And Eve took a taste, and she offered it to Adam,
And Adam wasn't able to refuse;
So he took a bite, and they both sat down
And ate the forbidden fruit.—
Back there, six thousand years ago,
Man first fell by woman—
Lord, and he's doing the same today.

And that's how sin got into this world.
And man, as he multiplied on the earth,
Increased in wickedness and sin.

He went on down from sin to sin,
From wickedness to wickedness,
Murder and lust and violence,
All kinds of fornications,
Till the earth was corrupt and rotten with flesh,
An abomination in God's sight.

And God was angry at the sins of men.
And God got sorry that he ever made man.
And he said: I will destroy him.
I'll bring down judgment on him with a flood.
I'll destroy ev'rything on the face of the earth,
Man, beasts and birds, and creeping things.
And he did—
Ev'rything but the fishes.

But Noah was a just and righteous man.
Noah walked and talked with God.
And, one day, God said to Noah,
He said: Noah, build thee an ark.
Build it out of gopher wood.
Build it good and strong.
Pitch it within and pitch it without.
And build it according to the measurements
That I will give to thee.
Build it for you and all your house,
And to save the seeds of life on earth;
For I'm going to send down a mighty flood
To destroy this wicked world.

And Noah commenced to work on the ark.
And he worked for about one hundred years.
And ev'ry day the crowd came round
To make fun of Old Man Noah.
And they laughed and they said: Tell us, old man,
Where do you expect to sail that boat
Up here amongst the hills?

But Noah kept on a-working.
And ev'ry once in a while Old Noah would stop,
He'd lay down his hammer and lay down his saw,
And take his staff in hand;
And with his long, white beard a-flying in the wind,
And the gospel light a-gleaming from his eye,
Old Noah would preach God's word:

Sinners, oh, sinners,
Repent, for the judgment is at hand.
Sinners, oh, sinners,
Repent, for the time is drawing nigh.
God's wrath is gathering in the sky.
God's a-going to rain down rain on rain.
God's a-going to loosen up the bottom of the deep,
And drown this wicked world.
Sinners, repent while yet there's time
For God to change his mind.

Some smart young fellow said: This old man's
Got water on the brain.
And the crowd all laughed—Lord, but didn't they laugh;
And they paid no mind to Noah,
But kept on sinning just the same.

One bright and sunny morning,
Not a cloud nowhere to be seen,
God said to Noah: Get in the ark!
And Noah and his folks all got in the ark,
And all the animals, two by two,
A he and a she marched in.
Then God said: Noah, bar the door!
And Noah barred the door.

And a little black spot begun to spread,
Like a bottle of ink spilling over the sky;
And the thunder rolled like a rumbling drum;
And the lightning jumped from pole to pole;
And it rained down rain, rain, rain,
Great God, but didn't it rain!
For forty days and forty nights
Waters poured down and waters gushed up;
And the dry land turned to sea.
And the old ark-a she begun to ride;
The old ark-a she begun to rock;
Sinners came a-running down to the ark;
Sinners came a-swimming all round the ark;
Sinners pleaded and sinners prayed—

Sinners wept and sinners wailed—
But Noah'd done barred the door.

And the trees and the hills and the mountain tops
Slipped underneath the waters.
And the old ark sailed that lonely sea—
For twelve long months she sailed that sea,
A sea without a shore.

Then the waters begun to settle down,
And the ark touched bottom on the tallest peak
Of old Mount Ararat.
The dove brought Noah the olive leaf,
And Noah when he saw that the grass was green,
Opened up the ark, and they all climbed down,
The folks, and the animals, two by two,
Down from the mount to the valley.
And Noah wept and fell on his face
And hugged and kissed the dry ground.

And then—

God hung out his rainbow cross the sky,
And he said to Noah: That's my sign!
No more will I judge the world by flood—
Next time I'll rain down fire.

The Crucifixion

THE CRUCIFIXION

Jesus, my gentle Jesus,
Walking in the dark of the Garden—
The Garden of Gethsemane,
Saying to the three disciples:
Sorrow is in my soul—
Even unto death;
Tarry ye here a little while,
And watch with me.

Jesus, my burdened Jesus,
Praying in the dark of the Garden—
The Garden of Gethsemane.
Saying: Father,
Oh, Father,
This bitter cup,
This bitter cup,
Let it pass from me.

Jesus, my sorrowing Jesus,
The sweat like drops of blood upon his brow,
Talking with his Father,
While the three disciples slept,
Saying: Father,
Oh, Father,
Not as I will,
Not as I will,
But let thy will be done.

Oh, look at black-hearted Judas—
Sneaking through the dark of the Garden—
Leading his crucifying mob.
Oh, God!
Strike him down!
Why *don't* you strike him down,
Before he plants his traitor's kiss
Upon my Jesus' cheek?

And they take my blameless Jesus,
And they drag him to the Governor,
To the mighty Roman Governor.
Great Pilate seated in his hall,—
Great Pilate on his judgment seat,
Said: In this man I find no fault.
I find no fault in him.
And Pilate washed his hands.

But they cried out, saying:
Crucify him!—
Crucify him!—
Crucify him!—
His blood be on our heads.
And they beat my loving Jesus,
They spit on my precious Jesus;
They dressed him up in a purple robe,
They put a crown of thorns upon his head,
And they pressed it down—
Oh, they pressed it down—
And they mocked my sweet King Jesus.

Up Golgotha's rugged road
I see my Jesus go.
I see him sink beneath the load,
I see my drooping Jesus sink.
And then they laid hold on Simon,
Black Simon, yes, black Simon;
They put the cross on Simon,
And Simon bore the cross.

On Calvary, on Calvary,
They crucified my Jesus.
They nailed him to the cruel tree,
And the hammer!
The hammer!
The hammer!

Rang through Jerusalem's streets.
The hammer!
The hammer!
The hammer!
Rang through Jerusalem's streets.

Jesus, my lamb-like Jesus,
Shivering as the nails go through his hands;
Jesus, my lamb-like Jesus,
Shivering as the nails go through his feet.
Jesus, my darling Jesus,
Groaning as the Roman spear plunged in his side;
Jesus, my darling Jesus,
Groaning as the blood came spurting from his wound.
Oh, look how they done my Jesus.

Mary,
Weeping Mary,
Sees her poor little Jesus on the cross.
Mary,
Weeping Mary,
Sees her sweet, baby Jesus on the cruel cross,
Hanging between two thieves.

And Jesus, my lonesome Jesus,
Called out once more to his Father,
Saying:
My God,

My God,
Why hast thou forsaken me?
And he drooped his head and died.

And the veil of the temple was split in two,
The midday sun refused to shine,
The thunder rumbled and the lightning wrote
An unknown language in the sky.
What a day! Lord, what a day!
When my blessed Jesus died.

Oh, I tremble, yes, I tremble,
It causes me to tremble, tremble,
When I think how Jesus died;
Died on the steeps of Calvary,
How Jesus died for sinners,
Sinners like you and me.

LET MY PEOPLE GO

And God called Moses from the burning bush,
He called in a still, small voice,
And he said: Moses—Moses—
And Moses listened,
And he answered and said:
Lord, here am I.

And the voice in the bush said: Moses,
Draw not nigh, take off your shoes,
For you're standing on holy ground.
And Moses stopped where he stood,
And Moses took off his shoes,
And Moses looked at the burning bush,
And he heard the voice,
But he saw no man.

Then God again spoke to Moses,
And he spoke in a voice of thunder:
I am the Lord God Almighty,
I am the God of thy fathers,
I am the God of Abraham,
Of Isaac and of Jacob.
And Moses hid his face.

And God said to Moses:
I've seen the awful suffering
Of my people down in Egypt.
I've watched their hard oppressors,
Their overseers and drivers;
The groans of my people have filled my ears
And I can't stand it no longer;
So I'm come down to deliver them
Out of the land of Egypt,
And I will bring them out of that land
Into the land of Canaan;
Therefore, Moses, go down,
Go down into Egypt,
And tell Old Pharaoh
To let my people go.

And Moses said: Lord, who am I
To make a speech before Pharaoh?
For, Lord, you know I'm slow of tongue.
But God said: I will be thy mouth and I will be thy tongue;
Therefore, Moses, go down,

Go down yonder into Egypt land,
And tell Old Pharaoh
To let my people go.

And Moses with his rod in hand
Went down and said to Pharaoh:
Thus saith the Lord God of Israel,
Let my people go.

And Pharaoh looked at Moses,
He stopped still and looked at Moses;
And he said to Moses: Who is this Lord?
I know all the gods of Egypt,
But I know no God of Israel;
So go back, Moses, and tell your God,
I will not let this people go.

Poor Old Pharaoh,
He knows all the knowledge of Egypt,
Yet never knew—
He never knew
The one and the living God.
Poor Old Pharaoh,
He's got all the power of Egypt,
And he's going to try
To test his strength
With the might of the great Jehovah,
With the might of the Lord God of Hosts,

The Lord mighty in battle.
And God, sitting high up in his heaven,
Laughed at poor Old Pharaoh.

And Pharaoh called the overseers,
And Pharaoh called the drivers,
And he said: Put heavier burdens still
On the backs of the Hebrew Children.
Then the people chode with Moses,
And they cried out: Look here, Moses,
You've been to Pharaoh, but look and see
What Pharaoh's done to us now.
And Moses was troubled in mind.

But God said: Go again, Moses,
You and your brother, Aaron,
And say once more to Pharaoh,
Thus saith the Lord God of the Hebrews,
Let my people go.
And Moses and Aaron with their rods in hand
Worked many signs and wonders.
But Pharaoh called for his magic men,
And they worked wonders, too.
So Pharaoh's heart was hardened,
And he would not,
No, he would not
Let God's people go.

And God rained down plagues on Egypt,
Plagues of frogs and lice and locusts,
Plagues of blood and boils and darkness,
And other plagues besides.
But ev'ry time God moved the plague
Old Pharaoh's heart was hardened,
And he would not,
No, he would not
Let God's people go.
And Moses was troubled in mind.

Then the Lord said: Listen, Moses,
The God of Israel will not be mocked,
Just one more witness of my power
I'll give hard-hearted Pharaoh.
This very night about midnight,
I'll pass over Egypt land,
In my righteous wrath will I pass over,
And smite their first-born dead.

And God that night passed over.
And a cry went up out of Egypt.
And Pharaoh rose in the middle of the night
And he sent in a hurry for Moses;
And he said: Go forth from among my people,
You and all the Hebrew Children;
Take your goods and take your flocks,
And get away from the land of Egypt.

And, right then, Moses led them out,
With all their goods and all their flocks;
And God went on before,
A guiding pillar of cloud by day,
And a pillar of fire by night.
And they journeyed on in the wilderness,
And came down to the Red Sea.

In the morning,
Oh, in the morning,
They missed the Hebrew Children.
Four hundred years,
Four hundred years
They'd held them down in Egypt land.
Held them under the driver's lash,
Working without money and without price.
And it might have been Pharaoh's wife that said:
Pharaoh—look what you've done.
You let those Hebrew Children go,
And who's going to serve us now?
Who's going to make our bricks and mortar?
Who's going to plant and plow our corn?
Who's going to get up in the chill of the morning?
And who's going to work in the blazing sun?
Pharaoh, tell me that!

And Pharaoh called his generals,
And the generals called the captains,
And the captains called the soldiers.

And they hitched up all the chariots,
Six hundred chosen chariots of war,
And twenty-four hundred horses.
And the chariots all were full of men,
With swords and shields
And shiny spears
And battle bows and arrows.
And Pharaoh and his army
Pursued the Hebrew Children
To the edge of the Red Sea.

Now, the Children of Israel, looking back,
Saw Pharaoh's army coming.
And the rumble of the chariots was like a thunder storm,
And the whirring of the wheels was like a rushing wind,
And the dust from the horses made a cloud that darked
    the day,
And the glittering of the spears was like lightnings in the
    night.

And the Children of Israel all lost faith,
The Children of Israel all lost hope;
Deep Red Sea in front of them
And Pharaoh's host behind.
And they mumbled and grumbled among themselves:
Were there no graves in Egypt?
And they wailed aloud to Moses and said:
Slavery in Egypt was better than to come
To die here in this wilderness.

But Moses said:
Stand still! Stand still!
And see the Lord's salvation.
For the Lord God of Israel
Will not forsake his people.
The Lord will break the chariots,
The Lord will break the horsemen,
He'll break great Egypt's sword and shield,
The battle bows and arrows;
This day he'll make proud Pharaoh know
Who is the God of Israel.

And Moses lifted up his rod
Over the Red Sea;
And God with a blast of his nostrils
Blew the waters apart,
And the waves rolled back and stood up in a pile,
And left a path through the middle of the sea
Dry as the sands of the desert.
And the Children of Israel all crossed over
On to the other side.

When Pharaoh saw them crossing dry,
He dashed on in behind them—
Old Pharaoh got about half way cross,
And God unlashed the waters,
And the waves rushed back together,
And Pharaoh and all his army got lost,
And all his host got drownded.

And Moses sang and Miriam danced,
And the people shouted for joy,
And God led the Hebrew Children on
Till they reached the promised land.

Listen!—Listen!
All you sons of Pharaoh.
Who do you think can hold God's people
When the Lord God himself has said,
Let my people go?

THE JUDGMENT DAY

In that great day,
People, in that great day,
God's a-going to rain down fire.
God's a-going to sit in the middle of the air
To judge the quick and the dead.

Early one of these mornings,
God's a-going to call for Gabriel,
That tall, bright angel, Gabriel;
And God's a-going to say to him: Gabriel,
Blow your silver trumpet,
And wake the living nations.

And Gabriel's going to ask him: Lord,
How loud must I blow it?
And God's a-going to tell him: Gabriel,
Blow it calm and easy.

Then putting one foot on the mountain top,
And the other in the middle of the sea,
Gabriel's going to stand and blow his horn,
To wake the living nations.

Then God's a-going to say to him: Gabriel,
Once more blow your silver trumpet,
And wake the nations underground.

And Gabriel's going to ask him: Lord
How loud must I blow it?

And God's a-going to tell him: Gabriel,
Like seven peals of thunder.
Then the tall, bright angel, Gabriel,
Will put one foot on the battlements of heaven
And the other on the steps of hell,
And blow that silver trumpet
Till he shakes old hell's foundations.

And I feel Old Earth a-shuddering—
And I see the graves a-bursting—
And I hear a sound,
A blood-chilling sound.
What sound is that I hear?
It's the clicking together of the dry bones,

Bone to bone—the dry bones.
And I see coming out of the bursting graves,
And marching up from the valley of death,
The army of the dead.
And the living and the dead in the twinkling of an eye
Are caught up in the middle of the air,
Before God's judgment bar.

Oh-o-oh, sinner,
Where will you stand,
In that great day when God's a-going to rain down fire?
Oh, you gambling man—where will you stand?
You whore-mongering man—where will you stand?
Liars and backsliders—where will you stand,
In that great day when God's a-going to rain down fire?

And God will divide the sheep from the goats,
The one on the right, the other on the left.
And to them on the right God's a-going to say:
Enter into my kingdom.
And those who've come through great tribulations,
And washed their robes in the blood of the Lamb,
They will enter in—
Clothed in spotless white,
With starry crowns upon their heads,
And silver slippers on their feet,
And harps within their hands;—

And two by two they'll walk
Up and down the golden street,
Feasting on the milk and honey
Singing new songs of Zion,
Chattering with the angels
All around the Great White Throne.

And to them on the left God's a-going to say:
Depart from me into everlasting darkness,
Down into the bottomless pit.
And the wicked like lumps of lead will start to fall,
Headlong for seven days and nights they'll fall,
Plumb into the big, black, red-hot mouth of hell,
Belching out fire and brimstone.
And their cries like howling, yelping dogs,
Will go up with the fire and smoke from hell,
But God will stop his ears.

Too late, sinner! Too late!
Good-bye, sinner! Good-bye!
In hell, sinner! In hell!
Beyond the reach of the love of God.

And I hear a voice, crying, crying:
Time shall be no more!
Time shall be no more!
Time shall be no more!
And the sun will go out like a candle in the wind,

The moon will turn to dripping blood,
The stars will fall like cinders,
And the sea will burn like tar;
And the earth shall melt away and be dissolved,
And the sky will roll up like a scroll.
With a wave of his hand God will blot out time,
And start the wheel of eternity.

Sinner, oh, sinner,
Where will you stand
In that great day when God's a-going to rain down fire?